MAX

The Life and Death of an Amazing Friend

SUSAN WHITLEY

Jacket and Book Design:
Humble Books
www.humblebooksmedia.com

Jacket and Interior Illustrations:
Fenne Kustermans
www.DOGvision.eu

ISBN 13 Paperback: 979-8-9948566-0-4
ISBN 13 Hardcover: 979-8-9948566-1-1

For Worldwide Distribution

To Cason and Cady,
who have taught me so much.

Hi, my name is Max.

MAX

I was born on Halloween...

...and went to live with my
family at Christmas.

I love chewing on things
and snuggling up tight.

Wearing sweaters,
t-shirts, jerseys and
pajamas is my favorite.

Costumes are not my favorite.

WV

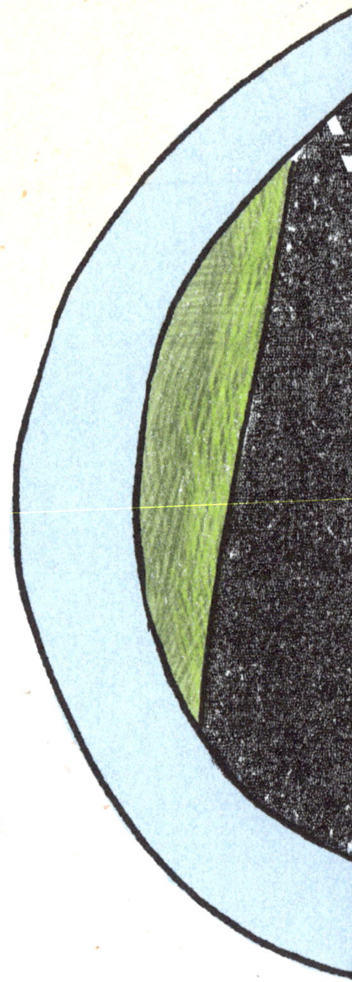

Ahhhh, riding in the car with my
head out the window.

Now, that's something
I love to do!

The Park, The Park, The Park!

We are going to the park!

I love to go walk around the park saying hello to other dogs and people.

But my favorite thing to do
is fetch my toy stick.

It gives me exercise and it is fun!

This is my life jacket.
It keeps me safe when
I go swimming!

I love to swim in
pools and in lakes.
My family loves to
go to the lake.

This is me getting older.

I don't run and play as much as I used to, but I love snuggling in my cozy blankets.

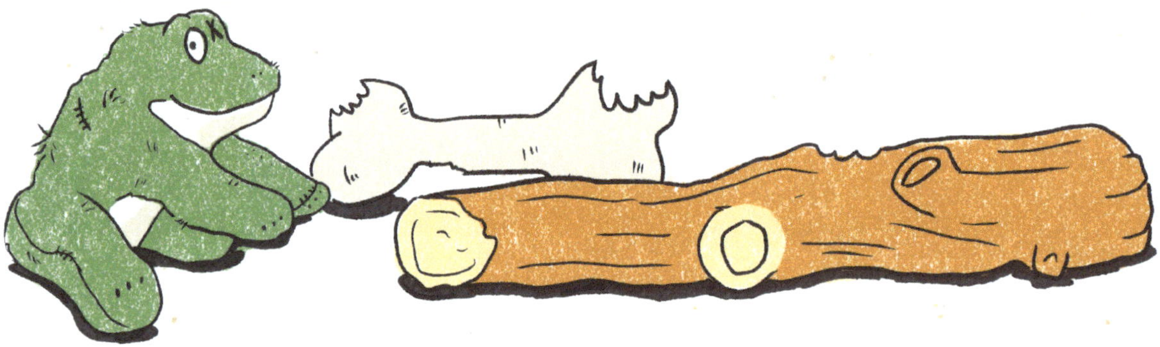

It makes me feel so good.

It's almost time for me to say goodbye.
I had a lot of fun and now it is time to go.

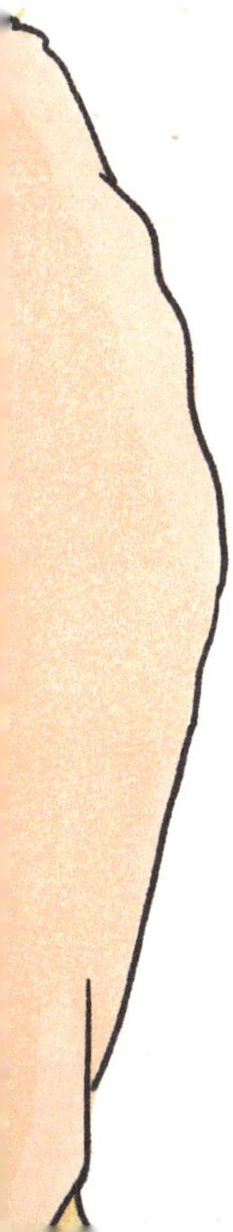

I hope my adventures
have made you smile.
They sure made me smile.

Max 10/31/2006 - 03/16/2019

You are worthy, O'Lord,
to receive glory and honor and power;
For you created all things,
and by Your will they exist
and were created.

REVELATION 4:11

DISCUSSION QUESTIONS

What memories in your life make you smile?

How can you make others smile?

ABOUT THE AUTHOR

Susan Whitley is a writer and aspiring author residing in Odessa, Texas. She is passionate about helping others find hope and healing through their own journeys. When not writing, she can be found spending time with her grandchildren, who help her see life through another perspective.

www.ingramcontent.com/pod-product-compliance
Ingram Content Group UK Ltd.
Pitfield, Milton Keynes, MK11 3LW, UK
UKHW061033310726
14089UKWH00010B/215
* 9 7 9 8 9 9 4 8 5 6 6 1 1 *